WITHDRAWN

AN ERITREAN

FAMILY

AN ERITREAN FAMILY

By Lois Anne Berg

Lerner Publications Company • Minneapolis

The interviews for this book were conducted in late 1994 and in 1995.

This book is available in two editions:
Library binding by Lerner Publications Company
Soft cover by First Avenue Editions
241 First Avenue North
Minneapolis, MN 55401
ISBN: 0-8225-3405-3 (lib. bdg.)
ISBN: 0-8225-9755-1 (pbk.)

A pronunciation guide can be found on page 62.

LIBRARY OF CONGRESS CATALOGING-IN-PUBLICATION DATA

Berg, Lois Anne.
 An Eritrean family / by Lois Anne Berg.
  p. cm. — (Journey between two worlds)
 Includes index.
 Summary: Describes an Eritrean family's struggle to emigrate from their country, which was fighting for independence from Ethiopia, to the United States and the adjustments they have made.
 ISBN 0-8225-3405-3 (lib. bdg. : alk. paper)
 1. Eritrean American families—Minnesota—Grand Rapids—Case studies—Juvenile literature. 2. Eritrean Americans—Minnesota—Grand Rapids—Case studies—Juvenile literature. 3. Refugees, Political—Minnesota—Grand—Rapids—Case studies—Juvenile literature. 4. Refugees, Political—Eritrea—Case studies—Juvenile literature. 5. Grand Rapids (Minn.)—Social life and customs—Juvenile literature. [1. Eritrean Americans. 2. Refugees.] I. Title. II. Series.
F614.G73 B47 1996
305.896/35077678—dc20   95-46970

Manufactured in the United States of America
1 2 3 4 5 6 – SP – 02 01 00 99 98 97

AUTHOR'S NOTE

I want to express my gratitude to Rezan and Fessahatsion Kiflu for taking a risk and sharing their private story with me. An extra special thanks goes to Yordanos Kiflu, who allowed me to tag along with her and her friends and who graciously answered all my questions.

The Kiflu family would like to thank those who have generously supported them in the United States. They include: the Refugee Committee in Grand Rapids, Minnesota; the congregation of Grand Rapids Zion Lutheran Church; Bob Herendeen; Peggy and Tim Landin; Andy and Marian Sjostrand; Bill and Ruth Williams; James and Mary Bake; Mary Zimmerli; Mark Stoltenburg; Nancy Hickman; Ann and Max Fulton; Tudy Motscheabosher; Karen O'Brien and Bonnie Schroeder; Jackie and Philip Solem; Charles and Lillian Lutterman; and Catherine McDonald.

Young friends (above) *play in a small village in Eritrea. War forced many Eritreans to become refugees* (facing page) *and to flee their East African homeland.*

SERIES INTRODUCTION

 What they have left behind is sometimes a living nightmare of war and hunger that most Americans can hardly begin to imagine. As refugees set out to start a new life in another country, they are torn by many feelings. They may wish they didn't have to leave their homeland. They may fear giving up the only life they have ever known. Many may also feel excitement and hope as they struggle to build a better life in a new country.

People who move from one place to another are called migrants. Two types of migrants are immigrants and refugees. Immigrants choose to leave their homelands, usually to improve their standards of living. They may be leaving behind poverty, famine (hunger), or a failing economy. They may be pursuing a better job or reuniting with family members.

Refugees, on the other hand, often have no choice but to flee their homeland to protect their own personal safety. How could anyone be in so much danger?

The government of his or her country is either unable or unwilling to protect its citizens from persecution, or cruel treatment. In many cases, the government is actually the cause of the persecution. Government leaders or another group within the country may be persecuting anyone of a certain race, religion, or ethnic background. Or they may persecute those who belong to a particular social group or who hold political opinions that are not accepted by the government.

From the 1950s through the mid-1970s, the number of refugees worldwide held steady at between 1.5 and 2.5 million. The number began to rise sharply in 1976. By the mid-1990s, it approached 20 million. These figures do not include people who are fleeing disasters

Camels cross a shallow inlet of the Red Sea, which borders Eritrea to the east. The country's narrow coastal desert is one of the hottest places in the world.

such as famine (estimated to be at least 10 million). Nor do they include those who are forced to leave their homes but stay within their own countries (about 27 million).

As this rise in refugees and other migrants continues, countries that have long welcomed newcomers are beginning to close their doors. Some U.S. citizens question whether the United States should accept refugees when it cannot even meet the needs of all its own people. On the other hand, experts point out that the number of refugees is small—less than 20 percent of all migrants worldwide—so refugees really don't have a very big impact on the nation. Still others suggest that the tide of refugees could be slowed through greater efforts to address the problems that force people to flee. There are no easy answers in this ongoing debate.

This book is one in a series called *Journey Between Two Worlds*, which looks at the lives of refugee families—their difficulties and triumphs. Each book describes the journey of a family from their homeland to the United States and how they adjust to a new life in America while still preserving traditions from their homeland. The series makes no attempt to join the debate about refugees. Instead, *Journey Between Two Worlds* hopes to give readers a better understanding of the daily struggles and joys of a refugee family.

Many Eritreans raise livestock, such as goats and camels.

 Fourteen-year-old Yordanos Kiflu is an eighth grader at Grand Rapids Middle School in northern Minnesota. She lives in Grand Rapids, a medium-sized town, with her mother, Rezan, her father, Fessahatsion (known as Kiflu), and her 18-year-old brother, Amanuel. Her four older sisters live in Minneapolis, which is Minnesota's largest city.

In 1987 the family came to the United States from Eritrea, which lies more than 7,000 miles (11,000 kilometers) from Minnesota. In fact, Eritrea is so far away that when Yordanos starts school at 8:00 A.M. in Grand Rapids, it's 5:00 P.M. and suppertime for her cousins in Eritrea. This country in northeastern Africa is surrounded on the north and west by Sudan. To the south lie Ethiopia and Djibouti. Eritrea's eastern coast borders the Red Sea.

In 1987, after several years in Sudanese refugee camps, Yordanos Kiflu and her family came to Grand Rapids, Minnesota.

Eritrea is located in northeastern Africa, a region known as the Horn of Africa. The name Eritrea comes from the Latin words for the Red Sea—Mare Erythraeum.

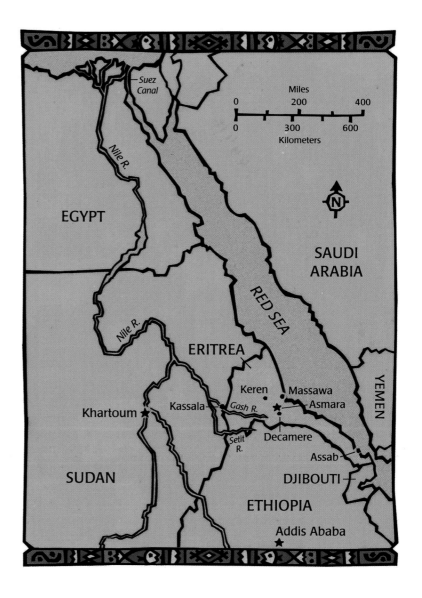

"How can I be Eritrean if I was born in Sudan?" Yordanos asks her mother, who is brushing her daughter's long, black hair.

"You are Eritrean because your father and I are," Rezan answers.

"I am also an American citizen," adds Yordanos.

"You're lucky," says Rezan as she ties back Yordanos's hair. "When you are an adult, you will be able to choose where you live. War made our choices."

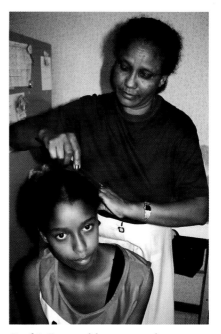

(Left) *Seated between her mother, Rezan, and her father, Kiflu, Yordanos is the youngest member of her family.* (Above) *Rezan brushes Yordanos's hair.*

From the early 1960s until the early 1990s, Eritrean guerrilla soldiers fought a bloody war for independence from Ethiopia. Because of this war, Yordanos's family and more than 750,000 other Eritreans were forced to leave their homeland. In 1991, when the Eritreans defeated the Ethiopians, people in Eritrea sang and danced in the streets for many days. For the first time in their history, the Eritreans were free.

But Ethiopia and many other countries around the world did not believe most Eritreans wanted the freedom the guerrillas had won. To convince the world, the Eritreans held an election in April 1993. Voters had to choose whether they wanted Eritrea to be a free country or to go back to being part of Ethiopia.

Because so many Eritreans were refugees and did not live in their homeland, the United Nations (an organization that works for world peace) set up voting stations all over the world. Yordanos's mother and father, for example, voted in Minneapolis. Almost 100 percent of the people who voted chose independence, and on May 28, 1993, Eritrea became an official nation.

A group of Eritrean voters holds up their Eritrean identification cards at the polls. Of the people who voted in the 1993 election, 99.8 percent chose independence for Eritrea.

Waving Eritrea's colors, a young man celebrates his country's independence from Ethiopia.

Rugged highlands dominate much of Eritrea.

 Eritrea is a small, mountainous country. Most Eritreans—about 80 percent—are farmers and herders. The herders raise cows, goats, and camels, while farmers grow cotton, potatoes, peanuts, and grains such as durra, maize (corn), and millet. The other 20 percent of the population live and work in cities.

Eritrea has nine different ethnic groups, each speaking its own language. Most people are either Christians or Muslims, who practice the religion of Islam.

On a map, Eritrea looks something like a hatchet. The wide western half of the country forms the blade of the hatchet. Across this hot and fertile lowland flow the Gash and the Setit Rivers. Resembling the long handle of a hatchet, the eastern part of Eritrea is a narrow strip of land along the Red Sea. This coastal lowland is one of the hottest places on earth, with temperatures often reaching 120° F (49° C) and higher.

Farmers in east central Eritrea harvest corn.

Built by the Italians in the late 1800s,
Eritrea's capital city of Asmara (right)
features wide boulevards lined with
palm trees and gardens. Northeast
of Asmara, huge cargo vessels
(above) dock at Massawa,
Eritrea's largest port.

With little rain and a hot climate, much of the land in eastern Eritrea is desert. Droughts (long periods without rain) occur about once every 10 years. Because crops won't grow during a drought, people usually prepare for them by putting aside enough food to survive the dry spells.

Although few people live in eastern Eritrea, two major port cities—Massawa and Assab—are located along the coast. For centuries, merchants in these ports have traded with neighboring countries.

Asmara, the capital city, is built on a plateau (highland) in south central Eritrea. Nearby is Keren, the country's second largest city. Yordanos's parents are from Decamere, a small town south of Asmara.

Since ancient times, outsiders have been coming into Eritrea. Some groups settled peacefully among the local inhabitants. Invaders from the Middle East and Abyssinia (now called Ethiopia) came for food, animals, and gold. The invaders also burned down houses and killed many Eritreans.

Until 1889 the Eritreans were never totally conquered, nor, until 1993, totally free. In the last 400 years, they have been ruled by a variety of outsiders—from the Ottoman Turks to the Egyptians, the Italians, the British, and lastly the Ethiopians.

In 1517 the Ottoman Turks captured the port of Massawa and controlled trade along the Red Sea coast for the next 300 years. But the Turks never ruled the interior regions of Eritrea. These areas were independent and governed by their own chiefs. Some parts were loosely controlled by neighboring Abyssinians.

The Ottoman Turks conquered coastal lands along the Red Sea in the 1500s. With control of ports such as Massawa, the Ottomans controlled trade in the region for many years.

Haile Selassie became emperor of Ethiopia in 1930.

The Turks gave the Egyptians control of Massawa in 1848. Using the port as their base, the Egyptians raided the interior of Eritrea and slowly spread their influence. In 1869 the Suez Canal opened in Egypt. This new water route linked the Mediterranean Sea to the Red Sea. Suddenly Eritrean ports were important. From these ports, valuable African goods could be shipped easily to Europe.

Most African countries at this time were controlled by Europeans. By 1885 the Italian army had forced the Egyptians out of Assab and Massawa. After many bloody battles, the Italians occupied all of Eritrea. In 1889 Italy and Ethiopia signed the Treaty of Uccialli, which established Eritrea's borders.

While governing Eritrea, the Italians took land from Eritreans to build plantations (big farms) for growing coffee, cotton, and fruit. The Italians used Eritrean workers to do the hard labor on these farms and to build roads, railways, large homes, factories, and parks. In Asmara Eritreans were not allowed to walk on the main street. Some shops even had separate entrances for Eritreans.

In 1936 Italy conquered Ethiopia. The emperor of Ethiopia, Haile Selassie, fled the country. Soon afterward, World War II (1939–1945) broke out in Europe and quickly spread to many other regions of the world. When Italy joined forces with Germany, Great Britain—

which was fighting against Germany and Italy—decided to help Ethiopia.

In 1941 the British and the Ethiopians defeated the Italians in Ethiopia and Eritrea. Haile Selassie returned to rule Ethiopia, and for the next 10 years, the British ran Eritrea.

By 1952 the British had decided it was too expensive to govern Eritrea, so they left the colony. The Eritreans asked the United Nations (UN) for independence. The United States, however, convinced the UN to create a federation, or partnership, between Ethiopia and Eritrea instead.

Yordanos's father and mother were in grade school in Asmara at that time.

An Eritrean gun crew works under the gaze of Italian officers in 1935, during Italy's campaign to conquer Ethiopia.

"Haile Selassie took over our radio stations and post offices and closed down our newspapers," Kiflu remembers. The thought still sparks anger in his eyes.

"He dismantled all our factories and transferred them to Addis Ababa [the capital of Ethiopia] and took control of our seaports," he continues.

"Haile Selassie was a tyrant," adds Rezan. "He forbade us to speak or write our language, Tigrinya. Books written in Tigrinya were burned. All Eritrean teachers were forced to teach Amharic [the language of Ethiopia], and lessons were conducted in Amharic. If the teachers refused, they were fired. When people have no jobs and no language, it means death to them."

 The Eritreans' yearning for freedom was strong. They held demonstrations and strikes. At one demonstration in 1958, Eritrean workers came together to protest Ethiopian rule. After three days, Haile Selassie ordered his army to shoot the protesters, and many people were killed. This only made Eritreans angrier. For safety they began to hide their resistance efforts.

In 1961 the Eritrean Liberation Front (ELF) was established to fight against Ethiopian rule. The ELF grew quickly but did not have enough money and weapons

In the 1950s, many Eritreans openly demonstrated against Ethiopian rule.

at first to lead a major attack against the Ethiopians. After some years, dissatisfied members of the ELF formed their own group called the Eritrean People's Liberation Front (EPLF).

In 1962 Ethiopians voted to end the federation. Against its wishes, Eritrea became a province of Ethiopia. Because only the UN had the official right to end the federation, the election was considered illegal. But the UN did not protest.

In the 1970s, Ethiopia was suffering from a severe drought and famine (extreme shortage of food). Emperor Haile Selassie tried to ignore the problem, not wanting other nations to know of the problems facing

Seeking freedom for Eritrea, the Eritrean People's Liberation Front (EPLF) began fighting against the Ethiopian army in the 1960s. As the EPLF gained ground during the late 1970s, they captured many Ethiopian soldiers (above) *as prisoners of war.*

25

(Above) *Mengistu Haile Mariam rose to power after Haile Selassie was overthrown in 1974.* (Facing page) *Refugee women and their children wait for food at an emergency station in Sudan. Drought and famine struck much of northeastern Africa— including Eritrea—several times during the 1970s and 1980s. Hundreds of thousands of refugees from both Eritrea and Ethiopia fled to eastern Sudan, where food and medical aid were available.*

his country. As a result of his silence, tens of thousands of people starved to death. In September 1974, a group of military leaders arrested Haile Selassie and put an end to his rule. Eventually a military leader named Mengistu Haile Mariam took control of Ethiopia.

"Life under Mengistu was even worse," Rezan says. "If you were Eritrean, he'd shoot you. He also burned our crops and houses and killed our animals."

"You see," Kiflu adds, "if all Eritreans died, Mengistu would get the land. He cared nothing for our people. All he wanted were the seaports. Without them Ethiopia would be landlocked and wouldn't have access to trade on the Red Sea."

Eritreans loved their land and were not willing to give it up without a fight. They continued their attacks and by 1978, the EPLF controlled almost 90 percent of Eritrea.

But Mengistu convinced the Soviet Union to support the Ethiopian army. The Soviets sent soldiers, military advisers, weapons, and fighter jets to Ethiopia.

All odds were against the Eritreans. They had no money, all their soldiers were volunteers, no country offered military support, and the only weapons they had were seized from Ethiopians during the fighting. The war grew, and thousands of Eritreans were killed or forced to run for their lives to Sudan.

In the spring of 1978, Yordanos's family was living in the town of Keren when Ethiopian soldiers came.

Yordanos hadn't been born yet when her family had to flee Eritrea, but she has heard the story of their flight many times.

"One evening I was walking down a dusty road in Keren," her father begins. "A friend called to me, 'Kiflu, I have come to warn you! Ethiopian soldiers from Asmara are coming to arrest you and other people they think are helping the EPLF. They're only 12 miles [20 kilometers] away. If they find you, they will kill you and your children!'

"My heart pounded. I thanked my friend for informing me, and I ran to the bank to withdraw our savings. But the bank was closed. Luckily some friends agreed to give me $400. That was enough money to rent two camels. You see, because of the war, there were no buses or cars. All gasoline was being used by the soldiers, and the few roads we had in Eritrea had been destroyed. Besides, all the roadways were guarded by the Ethiopian army. We put our lives into the hands of the camel drivers, who knew the lay of the land by heart.

"The camel drivers said, 'We leave when it is dark,'" continues Kiflu. "'Don't take anything but your bodies. We can't load the camels with things. The way to Sudan is long and hard.'

"I ran to the hospital to get your mother. She was cooking food and washing linens for wounded Eritrean soldiers. 'Rezan, come quickly!' I shouted. 'We have to leave our country. Now.'"

Rezan and Kiflu ran home to get their young daughters—Mulu (10), Elsa (8), Terhas (5), and Senait (3)—and their baby boy, Amanuel (1). By the time Rezan had packed a few oranges and a small bottle of water, the drivers were knocking at the door. Rezan began to bundle the children in jackets.

Kiflu describes how he and his family fled Eritrea, narrowly escaping Ethiopian soldiers.

Yordanos listens as Kiflu continues. "'Leave the jackets!' the camel drivers said. 'The soldiers are coming!'

'But how will we stay warm? What will we eat?' your mother asked.

"The camel drivers were firm. 'We'll take you and your children and just the clothes on their backs.'

"Luckily the weather was warm. Dressed only in their pajamas, Mulu and Elsa climbed onto the back of one of the kneeling camels outside our house. We worried about the younger children. If they went to sleep, they would fall off the other camel.

Led by experienced guides, the Kiflus traveled to Sudan on camelback. Camels can journey great distances with little food or water.

New soldiers in the EPLF undergo basic training. During the fight for independence, Eritrean leaders set up schools for the soldiers. The Eritreans knew that when freedom came, an educated population would be needed to rebuild their country.

"So your mother grabbed a sheet and tied Amanuel onto her belly, Terhas onto her right hip, and Senait onto her left hip. She tucked the small bottle of water into her dress. Then she straddled the kneeling camel and held on tightly as it leaned forward to stand up, first on its back legs and then on its front legs. Finally, with me walking alongside, we took off into the night.

"We knew the Ethiopian army outnumbered our fighters by ten to one. They had tanks, missiles, and automatic rifles, and they controlled our towns, roads, and the countryside. It was terrifying because they killed every person and animal they saw. Then they burned the houses and buildings. It was such a waste."

Fierce fighting and bomb attacks between the EPLF and Ethiopian soldiers caused heavy damage to Eritrea's cities and villages.

"Besides us, thousands of people from all over Eritrea were fleeing. Across the country, we fled in small groups of 25 or so. To avoid the Ethiopian soldiers, the camel drivers zigzagged back and forth through the forests and over the hills and mountains. For safety sometimes we had to go back where we had just come from. We never knew where we were, only that we were heading west to Sudan, the closest safe place.

"During the day, we hid under rocks, bushes, or thorny acacia trees. Those who did not hide became targets for Ethiopian fighter jets. They dropped cluster bombs or napalm bombs. Mostly we traveled at night, when the planes couldn't fly.

"One time we were traveling by day, when suddenly the camels dropped to their knees and began to crawl along the ground.

"'Go away! Go away!' the camel driver yelled to us. 'Hide in the trees!'

"Everyone jumped off the camels and crawled under the bushes, even the camels. Suddenly a fighter jet screamed out of the sky and dropped bombs on those who weren't hidden. We were very thankful to the camels. They could hear the planes from far away and were smart enough to hide," Kiflu says.

He continues the story, recalling how difficult it was to find food and water for his family during their long escape journey.

"A few times, the camel drivers sneaked into villages along the way and bought crackers or dried biscuits for us. Sometimes we saw a farmer with a cow and bought a little milk. But drinking the milk without boiling it first was dangerous. You could get sick. Your mother didn't dare light a fire to boil milk during the day because the smoke would give away our hiding place. And we couldn't build a fire at night because that's when we traveled. But it was okay traveling at night because we were too scared to sleep."

Tears well up in Kiflu's eyes as he continues speaking. "Many times we went all day and night without eating. Sometimes your mother had an orange and cut one slice for each child. Many times there was only enough for one bite each. Some of the children in the group cried, but your brothers and sisters didn't make a fuss. I think most of the time they were too frightened to eat or cry.

"As we headed over mountains and deserts, people stepped on poisonous snakes or scorpions and died. Sometimes we couldn't travel because of hyenas. They stalked the forests feeding on the dead animals and people.

"One evening the camel driver spoke to your mother and me. 'We are surrounded by enemy soldiers,' the driver said. 'In order to be safe, we must go over that mountain tonight.' He pointed ahead."

The Kiflus often went hungry as they made their way to Sudan. Sometimes they came across a farmer who would sell them some milk.

Tall mountains and rough terrain made the Kiflus' journey to Sudan very difficult.

"The mountain was as high as the clouds and went straight up. It looked impossible, but what choice did we have? As soon as it was dark, we all began to climb. The stones were smooth and slippery, and we all suffered cuts and bruises. Even the camels slid and fell.

"The night was black, and nobody could see anything. Once, your mother bumped into a boulder as big as a truck. She cried out just a little bit.

"'Shhh,' the driver scolded. 'No noise.'

"I was very frustrated and wished I had a flashlight for your mother, but they were forbidden. Even the smallest light could be seen from far away, and enemy soldiers shot at them in the dark.

"We crawled and climbed up that mountain, niche by niche, rock by rock. Finally, by morning, we had crossed safely."

"It took us two months to get out of Eritrea," says Kiflu. "On a map, it is about 500 miles [800 kilometers], but the way we crisscrossed the land, it's impossible to tell how far we traveled.

"At the border, I went into town to try to get papers to enter Sudan. By luck I saw a good friend.

"'Bring your family to my house,' my friend said.

"So we stayed with him and his wife for a few weeks until I was able to obtain papers to enter Sudan. He had a good house, good water, and food. We rested and regained our strength.

"While there I discovered that thousands of Eritreans were living in refugee camps in Sudan. I soon found work as a principal of an elementary school, and Rezan got a job teaching handicrafts at Suky—a refugee camp near Khartoum [Sudan's capital]. More than 8,000 refugees lived there."

Children in a refugee camp in Sudan learn to write on pieces of a paper bag.

Worried parents in a refugee camp watch over their sick child. Diseases spread quickly through the refugee camps in Sudan, killing thousands of Eritreans and Ethiopians.

"Is that where I was born?" Yordanos asks.

"Yes," Rezan replies, picking up the story. "That's the only good thing about that place. Even though I had a difficult time, you and your twin sister, Yorasialm, were born healthy and strong in 1981. But then disaster. When you were three months old, a measles epidemic hit the camp. You didn't get sick, but Yorasialm did, and she died. The disease was too strong, and the doctors and nurses couldn't do anything for her. It was a terrible, sad time. Many, many children died. I couldn't wait to leave that place.

"It was so hot and dry," Rezan remembers, "that by 10:00 in the morning, you couldn't step on the ground. The heat made me sick and I didn't feel like eating. And there were terrible dust storms. The high winds hit like a tornado, and the dust was so thick you couldn't see a person sitting right next to you. How I missed the clear skies of Eritrea!

"By the end of the year, your father had completed a nurses' training course offered in the camp. Then we moved to another refugee camp called Umgurgur, located near Kassala, a big city in Sudan. I had no idea we would be there for six years," says Rezan.

"That's where we had a goat," remembers Yordanos. "Amanuel and I used to chase it."

"Yes, she gave us milk," continues Rezan, smiling. "We lived in two round grass huts, which didn't have

Rezan remembers the family's life in Umgurgur—a refugee camp in northeastern Sudan.

Like these Eritrean refugees, the Kiflus lived in round grass huts while in the Sudanese refugee camps.

electricity. Every day a man led a donkey with a barrel of water strapped to its back into the camp. We bought the water for $5 a jug and stored it in a barrel at our house. Three jugs lasted only two days. It was very expensive. After some years, the Red Cross [an international aid organization] began to deliver free water in a tanker truck.

"We didn't have a refrigerator, so your father or I went to the market every day and bought fresh fruits and vegetables. We purchased fresh meat, too. Often we cut the meat into long strips and soaked them in oil and salt. Then we placed the strips out in the hot sun to dry. We stored the meat this way so it wouldn't spoil," explains Rezan.

At the camp, Rezan taught other Eritrean women how to sew and crochet. Because most of the women had never been to school, she also taught homemaking skills, hygiene, and nutrition.

"I showed the women how to cut and clean up the grass around their huts. This kept away the mosquitoes that carried malaria [a disease]," adds Rezan.

She continues her story, telling Yordanos what the children did while she was at work.

"During the morning, when I was teaching, you and Amanuel came with me to the women's center, where there was a day-care program for you and the children of the women attending classes. By the afternoon, the temperature reached more than 100° F [38° C], so all the schools would close. I'd bring you home to rest in the house until evening. Then you went out to play in the yard. The older children played soccer, volleyball, and basketball."

"I remember I had a plastic doll with blond hair," Yordanos adds.

"You took very good care of that doll," comments Rezan.

She continues, "Life was good for us. Your father worked as a nurse in a medical clinic built with money

(Left) *While in Sudan, Rezan and Kiflu shopped for fruit, vegetables, and meat at an outdoor market.* (Above) *The Kiflus and other refugees kept livestock such as sheep and goats, which provided fresh milk.*

raised by the Sudan Council of Churches. These churches from around the world provided money to pay workers and to buy food and medical supplies for the poorest refugees. The council even had schools for the older children. Your sisters attended an elementary school that was set up in camp. It was nice because the teachers were Eritrean and taught in our languages.

To help feed hungry refugees, countries around the world sent food aid to eastern Africa.

Eritrean children play among the crowded huts of a refugee camp.

boarding school in Kassala about 120 miles [190 kilometers] away."

"Why did we come to America then?" asks Yordanos.

"The war between Eritrea and Ethiopia kept getting worse, and we didn't know when there would be peace," explains Rezan. "Sudan is a poor country. School ended at tenth grade and there wasn't any kind of advanced training. Your father and I believed the only hope for your future was a good education. The best place for that was the United States. So in 1983, we applied for American visas. It took four years before we were allowed to leave."

Rezan reflects, "I felt guilty leaving my people behind with all their problems. Our fighters were just kids struggling by themselves. Many were friends, neighbors, and relatives. But you children were the future. I believed if you had a good education, you could go back to help Eritrea when there was peace. My friends told me that was a way of fighting, too."

THE TRUSTED COW

Yordanos's parents told the following story so she and her brother and sisters would learn that it is important to love and care for all people and to treat them in a kind manner. Kiflu saw Eritreans fighting for independence carry out the lessons of this story. He witnessed the soldiers give their food first to local women, children, and sick people. Then they fed prisoners of war. If there was anything left, the Eritrean soldiers ate. Usually it was only one small bite. By giving up concern for themselves, the Eritrean soldiers overcame tremendous obstacles and won freedom for their people and the children of future generations.

Once upon a time, on the highlands of eastern Africa, a man and his wife lived in a round hut with their young children and a black-and-white cow. Every day the mother milked the cow to feed her growing children. Suddenly the mother became very, very sick. She knew she was going to die. So she called the cow.

"Cow," she said, "please make a promise to feed my children. Soon I'm going to die, and they'll have no mother." Soon after the cow agreed to keep the promise, the mother died.

A few years later, the father met another woman and married her. They had a son. The woman loved her child very much and resented having to care for her lively stepchildren. To make sure her son grew strong, she saved the freshest milk for him. The milk she gave her stepchildren was spoiled.

But no matter how wicked the woman was, the stepchildren were always happy. Their noisy laughter annoyed the woman. So during the day, she sent them into the forest with the cow.

The cow remembered the promise it had made to the children's mother before she died. Every day the cow said to the children, "Come. Drink my warm, sweet milk."

Because they had been raised together, the children understood what the cow said. Every day they did as it asked. The rich, creamy milk made the stepchildren strong and healthy.

Years went by. One day the cruel step-

mother noticed how muscular her stepchildren were compared to her own son. "Why does my son grow weak when I have given him the best milk?" she asked.

The next day, she sent her son into the forest with the stepchildren and the cow.

"Watch them carefully," she said. "See what they do that makes them strong."

When they arrived at a grassy field, the cow stopped. "Come," it said to the children. "Drink my warm, sweet milk."

The stepchildren did as the cow asked. But their stepmother's son was too afraid to drink. He ran home and told his mother what he had seen.

The stepmother stomped her foot in anger. That night she pretended to be sick and went to bed early.

"What is the cause of this?" her husband asked.

"I want to eat the cow's meat," she said.

"That's impossible," the husband replied. "How can we kill the cow? Its milk nourishes our children." "If you don't kill the cow," the stepmother said, "I will die." The husband couldn't bear to lose another wife. So the next day, he killed the cow and butchered it. He roasted the meat and served it to his wife.

The days passed, and she got fatter and lazier feasting upon the meat of the cow. She didn't notice that her son and stepchildren were growing thinner and weaker. One morning, when there was nothing left of the cow but a pile of bones and four black hooves, the stepmother rose and looked about for her son. She found him and the other children huddled in a corner, dead.

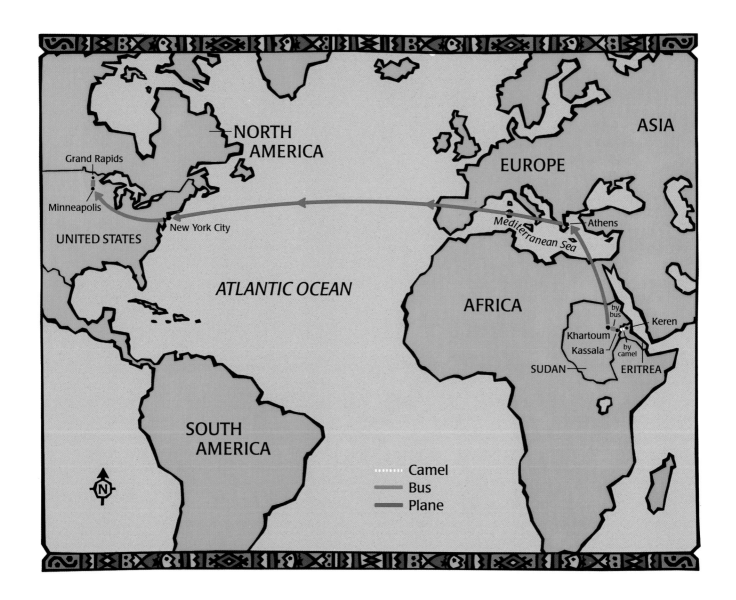

NORTH AMERICA

Grand Rapids

Minneapolis

UNITED STATES

New York City

ATLANTIC OCEAN

SOUTH AMERICA

EUROPE

ASIA

Mediterranean Sea

Athens

AFRICA

by bus

Keren

Khartoum

Kassala

by camel

SUDAN

ERITREA

Camel
Bus
Plane

N

Yordanos was six years old when she came to the United States in 1987. Made up of people from local churches, the Refugee Committee of Grand Rapids, Minnesota, sponsored the Kiflu family.

To come to Minnesota, Yordanos, her parents, her four sisters, and her brother boarded an airplane in Khartoum, Sudan. They were terrified at first. The only airplanes they knew about dropped bombs.

"The airplane food was really strange," Yordanos remembers. "They served hot dogs. I didn't know what they were so I didn't eat anything until we landed in Athens [the capital of Greece]. I ate some pasta there."

From Athens the family flew to New York and then to Minneapolis. Some Eritreans were at the Minneapolis airport to welcome another Eritrean family traveling with the Kiflus.

The Kiflus traveled by plane from Sudan to Minnesota.

Andy Sjostrand (above, with Kiflu) *helped the Kiflus get settled in Grand Rapids* (right) *and has remained a good friend of the family.*

"My parents knew one of the men in the welcoming party and were happy to see him," Yordanos says. "I just stayed close to my mother and didn't understand what was happening. At that time, I thought we were just coming for a visit. I didn't realize we were going to stay and live in the United States."

Yordanos continues, "After a couple of hours, we had to get onto another plane and head farther north. The other Eritreans stayed in Minneapolis. It was hard to leave everyone and go on to someplace else by ourselves."

When the Kiflus first arrived in Grand Rapids, they stayed at Camp Hiawatha, a local church camp.

"There was a pretty lake at that camp," says Yordanos. She smiles at the memory. "I ran into the water to catch the ducks. But I grew up in the desert of Sudan and had never seen a lake before. I didn't know how to swim and I didn't know lakes were deep. To keep me out of the water, my mom told me that a monster lived there!"

Eventually the Kiflu family settled into a house. They had been there a few days when a neighbor knocked on the door. The neighbor's daughter, Rachel, was the same age as Yordanos, and the woman wanted the girls to be friends.

Rachel was Yordanos's first friend in the United States.

Yordanos and her father read a newspaper from Eritrea. At home the Kiflus speak Tigrinya, a language used in Eritrea.

"The first time Yordanos came to my house, she didn't speak English. So we didn't talk," explains Rachel. "We just sat next to each other and played with Barbie dolls."

"Rachel's store-bought toys were neat, and I liked playing with them," says Yordanos. "Except for my doll, most of my toys in Sudan were homemade."

In Grand Rapids, the Kiflus' sponsors helped the family get the documents they needed to work in the United States.

"A lot of nice people helped us when we first came," Yordanos says. "But it was kind of weird because we were the only black family in town."

Because schooling in the Sudanese refugee camps didn't start until second grade, Yordanos had never been to school. To catch up to her American classmates, Yordanos attended kindergarten every day instead of every other day like the other students.

She and Amanuel, who was in second grade, stayed after school for tutoring in English. Yordanos speaks English without an accent now. She remembers her teacher Ms. Fulton. But she doesn't remember learning the language.

Education is important to the Kiflus, so Yordanos is very serious about her studies. She takes a wide variety of classes in junior high, including woodshop (above). In the evenings, Yordanos works hard to complete her homework (left).

Yordanos and her friends try for a prize at a carnival.

"I was in school all day every day, and everybody spoke only English. I think that helped me learn quickly," Yordanos says. "After school I played with Rachel. That helped, too."

Rachel adds, "At first, when Yordanos talked to me, she'd begin a sentence in English, and when she didn't know the words, she'd finish in her language!"

Yordanos remarks, "I got teased sometimes because of my race, but I have many friends now, and everyone at the junior high knows me. But I will always be different here in northern Minnesota."

AN ERITREAN WELCOME

When people in the United States see a friend, they say, "Hi! How are you?" Then they often shake hands, or slap a high five, or give a hug.

When Rezan meets an Eritrean friend, the two shake hands. One person says, *"Dehando hadirka,"* which means "How are you?" The other person replies, *"Emesgen Amlak,"* which means, "Thanks to God, I am okay." A less formal greeting, *selaam,* can be used to say hello or good-bye. It means "peace."

If they haven't seen each other for a long time, the friends touch right cheeks together, then left cheeks, and then right cheeks again. If the person is a really good friend, they kiss each other's cheeks.

Yordanos greets her young friend Lilly.

Rezan crochets blankets and makes other items ordered by friends.

Yordanos's mother had trouble finding work because she didn't speak English. After a few months, Rezan found a job washing dishes at a restaurant during the day, and she took English classes at night. To earn extra money, Rezan crocheted afghans (blankets) and doilies (small decorative mats) and sewed bunnies, dolls, and teddy bears ordered by friends. Her friend Bonnie loaned her a knitting machine so Rezan could make hats to sell. "That really helped support our family," Rezan says. "I will always be grateful to Bonnie."

Although Yordanos's father studied English in school and speaks the language well, he ran into problems finding work. Because he wasn't licensed to be a nurse in the United States, Kiflu had to go back to school for more training. Eventually he became a licensed nurse's aide and found a job at the local hospital.

Coming from the hot climate of Sudan, the Kiflus also had to make a major adjustment to the cold weather in northern Minnesota.

"Yordanos was always cold," says her friend Rachel. "I'd be in a T-shirt and shorts thinking it was hot, and Yordanos would be bundled up in jeans and a sweatshirt—freezing!"

The first snowfall took the family by surprise. "One morning we woke up and the ground was covered," recalls Kiflu. "Nobody told us about snow, and we had never seen it before. That day I had to buy boots and warm jackets for the whole family."

Rezan shovels the sidewalk in front of her family's house. Used to the hot, dry weather of eastern Africa, the Kiflus had to adjust to Minnesota's cold climate and heavy snowfalls.

In the United States, the Kiflus found large grocery stores with hundreds of food items they had never seen before. Frozen dinners, cake mixes, and instant puddings were all new to the family. But they discovered that Americans eat many of the same foods Eritreans do.

The traditional Eritrean food is *injera,* which is like a thin, spongy pancake. A stack of cold injera is placed in the middle of the table. Spiced foods, such as *zigny* (a sauce made with goat, lamb, beef, or chicken), stew, lentils, or vegetables are poured on top of the pile.

To eat injera, everybody sits around the table and helps themselves. First, people break off a piece of injera from the side of the stack. Then, using the injera as a spoon, they scoop up the food that has been placed on top and eat it with the injera. Yordanos likes this way of eating because there are few dishes to wash!

Yordanos chooses tea, while her parents and other adults like to drink *bun* (Eritrean coffee). In the United States, automatic pots brew coffee in minutes. But in Eritrea, making coffee is a social event. An Eritrean saying observes, "If you prepare coffee, something calls people to come."

The first step in making bun is to roast raw coffee beans in a pan on top of the stove. The smoking beans are shown to the guests so they can enjoy the aroma. Then the beans are ground.

The Kiflus enjoy preparing traditional Eritrean food, such as pancakelike injera, *which is topped with spiced sauces, stews, and vegetables.*

In Minnesota Rezan uses an electric grinder. In Eritrea she ground the beans by hand using a pestle (a small utensil for pounding or grinding) and mortar (a sturdy container). The ground coffee is then put into a round pot with a long, tubelike spout. Water is added, and the mixture is slowly brought to a boil.

When she came to Minnesota, Rezan ordered a special brazier (a small metal box that holds burning coals) to brew coffee outside in warm weather. In the winter, when it is cold and snowy, Rezan boils the coffee on her kitchen stove.

Preparing a strong coffee called bun *is a social event that starts with burning incense. Rezan makes bun by roasting the coffee beans on the stove* (left), *then boiling the ground coffee with water in a round pot* (middle). *She serves bun* (right) *to her guests in tiny cups with lots of sugar.*

In Eritrea the Kiflus belonged to the Ethiopian Orthodox Church, a branch of Christianity. During special celebrations, such as Easter (facing page), Orthodox priests (above) wear colorful robes.

 The Kiflus are Christians. They belong to Zion Lutheran Church in Grand Rapids. Like other Christians around the world, the Kiflus enjoy celebrating Christmas. They decorate a Christmas tree, and Yordanos's sisters come home from Minneapolis for the holiday. Family members exchange gifts and eat traditional Eritrean foods.

When they were children in Eritrea, Yordanos's parents belonged to the Ethiopian Orthodox Church, a branch of Christianity.

The Orthodox Church has a different calendar. The 12 months of the year each have 30 days. This leaves five extra days, which make up a short thirteenth month. When Eritrea was part of Ethiopia, this calendar was used throughout the country. Since independence, though, Eritreans have relied on the same calendar that is used in the United States.

Yordanos has made many friends in Grand Rapids, including Alicia (center) and Rachel (right). But Rezan and Kiflu miss their friends and family in Eritrea.

Living in the United States has been lonely for Kiflu and Rezan. They have no relatives here, and their closest Eritrean friends live three and a half hours away in Minneapolis. Once or twice a year, they get together for graduations or visiting. Then they cook traditional food, drink Eritrean coffee, and exchange news of their homeland.

Many people have helped the Kiflu family adjust to life in America. One of their most treasured gifts was from Rezan's friend Peggy Landin. When the war in Eritrea ended, Peggy sponsored Rezan's father so he could visit his daughter in the United States. He was 80 years old. It had been many years since Rezan had seen her father, and Yordanos had never met him.

"It was great meeting my grandfather," Yordanos says. "He knew a little English, and I knew a little Tigrinya, so we communicated well. Sometimes we watched television together. Once, he saw a Big Mac commercial on television and was surprised that one person could eat so much! It would have fed a whole family in Eritrea."

Yordanos, who is on the track team at school, relaxes with her friends after running hurdles.

Yordanos's grandfather told her about Eritrea's fight for independence and how much the people had sacrificed in that struggle. He told Yordanos about the land and urged her to stay connected to Eritrea by learning to speak and write their language well.

"I knew my grandfather and my parents had gone through a lot. I have always been proud of them, and I am proud to be Eritrean. But listening to my grandfather made everything real and gave me deeper roots," says Yordanos.

 The Kiflus have worked hard to make a good life in the United States. Many of their hopes for their family and for their homeland have come true. The war ended, and Eritrea is finally an independent country. And perhaps most importantly, their children are getting a good education.

Mulu, the eldest daughter, has gone to college in Minneapolis and now has an accounting job. Elsa, who works for a bank, is studying for an advanced degree in business. Terhas is studying cosmetology (beauty treatment of hair and skin), and Senait is in college studying dress design.

Yordanos's brother, Amanuel, is a junior in high school. He's a good student and works part-time to earn money for college.

On a cold winter day, Yordanos watches a snowstorm brew outside.

Yordanos hopes to go to college someday, too. She takes her studies seriously. "It's why we came here," she notes. Yordanos is also active in sports. In the spring, she runs distance events for the track team and in the fall, she runs on the cross-country team.

Because there is peace in Eritrea, Rezan and Kiflu would like to move back to their country. But the war destroyed their home and their village, leaving only rubble behind. The Kiflus do not have enough money to start over again in Eritrea. And their children are not finished with school yet. Going back to Eritrea remains one of their dreams. Considering the obstacles they have already overcome, it is very possible this dream will one day come true.

FURTHER READING

Courlander, Harold and Wolf Leslau. *The Fire on the Mountain and Other Stories from Ethiopia and Eritrea.* New York: Henry Holt & Co., 1995.

Ethiopia in Pictures. Minneapolis: Lerner Publications Company, 1993.

Kurtz, Jane. *Ethiopia: The Roof of Africa.* New York: Dillon Press, 1991.

Kurtz, Jane. *The Storyteller's Beads.* New York: Harcourt Brace & Co., 1997.

Kurtz, Jane. *Trouble.* New York: Harcourt Brace & Co., 1997.

Papstein, Robert. *Eritrea: Revolution at Dusk.* Trenton, New Jersey: Red Sea Press, 1991.

Pateman, Roy. *Even the Stones Are Burning.* Trenton, New Jersey: Red Sea Press, 1990.

Wilson, Amrit. *Women and the Eritrean Revolution.* Trenton, New Jersey: Red Sea Press, 1991.

PRONUNCIATION GUIDE

Amharic (am-HAHR-ihk)
Decamere (deh-kuhm-HAHR-ay)
Djibouti (juh-BOO-tee)
Eritrea (eh-REE-tray-uh)
Haile Selassie (HY-lee suh-LA-see)
Khartoum (kahr-TOOM)
Kiflu (KIH-floo)
Massawa (muh-SAH-wuh)
Mengistu Haile Mariam (mehn-GOOS-too HY-lee MEHR-ee-uhm)
Rezan (REH-zahn)
Suky (SOO-kee)
Terhas (tehr-HAHS)
Tigrinya (tuh-GREE-nyuh)
Yorasialm (yoh-RAH-see-ehlm)
Yordanos (yohr-DAHN-ohs)

Tigrinyan Words and Phrases
bun (BOON)
dehando hadirka (deh-HAHN-doh hah-DEHR-kuh)
emesgen Amlak (uh-MUHS-kihn uhm-LUHK)
injera (ihn-JEHR-uh)
selaam (suh-LAHM)
zigny (ZIHG-nee)

*The sounds of the languages of Africa are often difficult to translate into English. The pronunciations on this page are approximations.

INDEX

Abyssinia, 20
Addis Ababa, 24
Asmara, 18, 19, 22, 23
Assab, 19, 22

Britain, 20, 22, 23

camels, 8, 9, 16, 28, 30, 31, 32, 34
customs, beliefs, and traditions, 51, 54–55, 56

Decamere, 19
demonstrations and strikes, 24
Djibouti, 10
drought, 19, 25, 26

Egypt, 20, 22
Eritrea: borders and locations of, 10, 12; climate of, 8, 17, 19; escape from, 28–34, 44; ethnic groups of, 16; federation of, 23; history of, 20–27; independence of, 14, 24–26, 31, 60; jobs in, 16, 17, 19; map of, 12; origin of name, 12; schools in, 24, 31; topography of, 16, 17
Eritrean Liberation Front (ELF), 24–25
Eritrean People's Liberation Front (EPLF), 25, 26, 31, 32
Ethiopia, 10, 14, 20, 22–26, 41

famine, 9, 25–26
farmers, 16, 17, 22
folktale, 42–43
food, 33, 38, 54–55, 56, 59

Gash River, 17
goats, 9, 16, 37, 39
Grand Rapids (Minnesota), 10, 11, 45, 46, 48; climate of, 52–53; education in, 10, 48–50, 60–61; friends in, 46, 47–48, 50, 52, 58, 59; jobs in, 52

Haile Selassie, 22, 23, 24, 25–26

Italy, 20, 22, 23

Kassala, 37, 41
Keren, 19, 26, 28
Khartoum, 35, 45

language, 16, 24, 48, 51, 59, 60; learning English, 48, 50, 52

maps, 12, 44
Massawa, 18, 19, 20, 21, 22
Mengistu Haile Mariam, 26

Ottoman Turks, 20, 21, 22

Red Cross, 38

Red Sea, 8, 10, 17, 20, 21, 22, 26
refugee camps, 26, 35–41; jobs in, 35, 38, 39; schools in, 35, 38–39, 40–41, 48
Refugee Committee, 45
refugees, 6–9, 14
religion, 16, 56

Setit River, 17
Sudan, 10, 26, 35–36, 37, 38, 39, 41, 45; escape to, 28–35
Sudan Council of Churches, 40
Suky, 35

trade, 19, 20, 21, 22, 26

Uccialli, Treaty of, 22
Umgurgur, 37–41
United Nations, 14, 23, 25
United States, 9, 10, 23, 41, 45, 51

ABOUT THE AUTHOR

Lois Anne Berg moved to Asmara, the capital of Eritrea, in 1970 to be with her husband, who worked for the U.S. Army at Kagnew Station. During the two years she lived in Asmara, she gained tremendous respect for the Eritrean people. In 1980 Ms. Berg and her husband sponsored a young Eritrean woman, bringing her to live with them in the United States.

Ms. Berg is a writer who lives with her husband and three children in Pengilly, Minnesota. This is her first book for children. She feels honored to be able to tell a small part of the Eritrean story.

PHOTO ACKNOWLEDGMENTS

Cover photographs © Ed Kashi (left) and © Peter Ford (right). All inside photos by Peter Ford except the following: © Robert Papstein, pp. 6, 8, 9, 15, 16, 17, 18 (both), 19, 30, 31, 33, 34, 35, 40, 56, 57; © Ed Kashi, pp. 7, 32, 38, 41; Laura Westlund, pp. 12, 44; Lois Anne Berg, pp. 13 (right), 46 (left), 47, 50, 51, 54; Andrew Beswick, p. 14; Culture and Tourism Office of the Turkish Embassy, p. 21; Archive Photos/London Daily Express, p. 22; UPI/Bettmann, pp. 23, 26; Archive Photos, p. 24; Archive Photos/Pictorial Parade, p. 25; Reuters/Bettmann Newsphotos, pp. 27, 36; Jenny Matthews, p. 39 (both); Alycia Berg, p. 64; Textile cut-ins by Lois Anne Berg